W9-CFL-408

25 Meaningful Albums

25 Talented Artists Share Their Most Meaningful Scrapbooks

Copyright 2004 Chatterbox, LLC

All rights reserved

No part of this book may be reproduced or transmitted in any matter what-
soever without the written consent of the publisher, except as individual
copies for personal craft projects which are not for resale.

Any views expressed in the albums or essays are the sole responsibility of
the individual designer(s) and not a reflection of the views of Chatterbox.

Published by Chatterbox, LLC

The use of products and trademark names are for information purposes
only, with no intention of infringement upon those trademarks.

For information about bulk sales or promotional pricing, please contact
Customer Service at info@chatterboxinc.com.

1.888.416.6260

2141 W. Beacon Light Rd.
Eagle, Idaho 83616
www.chatterboxinc.com

Printed in USA

ISBN 1-892326-14-0

The Artists

The Meaning...

After hosting the first annual "Make It Meaningful Album Contest," we knew within days of the first entries arriving that these albums, and their accompanying stories, were destined and begging to be shared with the world.

Stepping into the lives and hearts of these 25 scrapbook artists was quite an experience for me. Choosing a grand prize winner was difficult, as you will understand after absorbing this book and its contents into your own heart. Each album is as different as the fingerprint of the artist.

Creating memory albums is one of the most selfless and priceless acts of love that I can think of. As you'll see in the pages ahead, these women (and one man!) created works of art and soul that could never be replaced. You'll be able to see their albums, as well as read the accounts of making their album, and what that experience meant to each of them. You'll read that each artist had a life-changing experience in making their album.

You will likely be inspired to create a meaningful album all of your own: to not let one more minute go by without having those things in your own life and

heart documented and preserved. Our hope is that you will act on that inspiration.

As you look through these albums, perhaps you'll even be inspired to enter our yearly contest with an album of your own! See our website at www.chatter-boxinc.com for the details. We'd love to come to your door this year!

Sincerely,

Melody Ross

Chatterbox

Vanessa Reyes

I created this album for my daughter in the event that I or my husband could not be there for her. We want her to always know that she is loved. "If For Any Reason" Mommy and Daddy are not around when she is faced with hardships, celebrating a special event, or conquering a milestone, she can open this album and read a letter from the both of us giving her advice, encouragement, knowledge, and wisdom. We are very fortunate to have the love of a large family. Each type of love is unique in one way or another, but there is no love that can compare or replace the love between a child and her parents. With this we are blessed and not a moment goes by without knowing it. These are some of the gifts we wanted to give her in a form she could hold on to, grow with, and read over and over again.

Each page in her album is dedicated to an event that she will most likely face in her lifetime. Also included on each page is an envelope enclosed with handwritten letters from her father and I. These letters are heartfelt and uncensored; we agreed not to read each other's writings as they will be a true and precious gift for her to unfold. These personal letters seemed to be the most difficult task for us to overcome. Though Hevani is just a child, we had to imagine and envision her at older stages in her life, then recreate our own personal trials and celebrations in order for us to give her the true feelings and emotions one might go through. We touched on subjects such as her first LOVE (a tough one for my husband, I could tell by his face while he was writing), her WEDDING day, and the BIRTH of her first

child. I also dedicated a page for her to come to whenever she felt lonely; the letters on this page are extremely important. We all know that growing up in this new generation is different than the one we are familiar with. This generation is far more violent, sexually mature, and disrespectful. Knowing this, my husband and I stressed in our letters the strength of an individual, and the love of a family.

Hevani will be three on New Years Eve, and though no one is promised a tomorrow, with this album we have given her the promise of always having a piece of us: always knowing that she is loved, and always feeling like she is wanted.

As I neared the completion of her album, I came to realize just what a gift we had created for her. I even felt a sense of ease, knowing that we had insured being a part of such a special life, and giving her a love unmeasured. This has been a true journey, far more than what I expected. This was a reward in itself!

Other things may change us, but we start and end with family.

—Anthony Brandt

Ruth De Fauw

songs
in the
key of me

I knew that this album was going to put me through some tough memories, but I was ready for it. I didn't know how to approach some of these topics in just a conventional album—it just seemed awkward in a regular "All about Me" approach, and it wasn't just all about ME. I'm not sure exactly how this theme of "Songs in the Key of Me" finally came about. My sister and I were talking one day about how each time we visited our dad's and he had the radio on, we would always end up hearing Superman—"Mom's song." Although we don't hear it as often anymore, it will end up being played at important moments in our lives, the last time during my daughter's birthday party. Lately I had been having the same experience with the song "Good Mother" by Jann Arden. This made me think of how my husband and I would always smile when the Dixie Chick's version of Fleetwood Mac's Landslide came out and was everywhere, because we had the original on our wedding CD in the year 2000. All these kinds of things were sticking out in my mind, and I started to list the songs in my life that meant so much to me. I discovered the soundtrack of my life.

I knew that I would be dealing with several difficult points in my life. My husband and my father's illnesses, which occurred at the same time, and the death of my mother. I wanted to have at least ONE place where I recorded these events because they had such a huge effect on my life. I knew that I had to get them down before my memory started to alter or forget the events. When I sat down and wrote the story of the last days of my Mother's life, it was with a box of Kleenex, and a need to be as honest as I could. I showed the story to my sister and areas that were hazy for me, she remembered crystal clear and she helped me to preserve the moment better. But I had to remember too, that this was MY story, It was my observances, opinions and feelings, and no one

else's. Another life altering event was the birth of my daughter Grace. How special and lucky was I to know unconditional love, and I was so happy that my mother got to meet Gracie, if only for a while

What I had hoped to be able to show with this album, especially to myself and my family, was that although these events happen, it will eventually be alright, that the horrible things just make the wonderful things even better! You can handle the hard things in life, and still believe in hope. The last two layouts in the book are in symbolic colors, the pictures are in color too. I wanted to show this feeling of recovering, being alive, and alert and thankful for what I have. These events and stages in my life made me who I am today, I have learned that I have so much to look forward to…

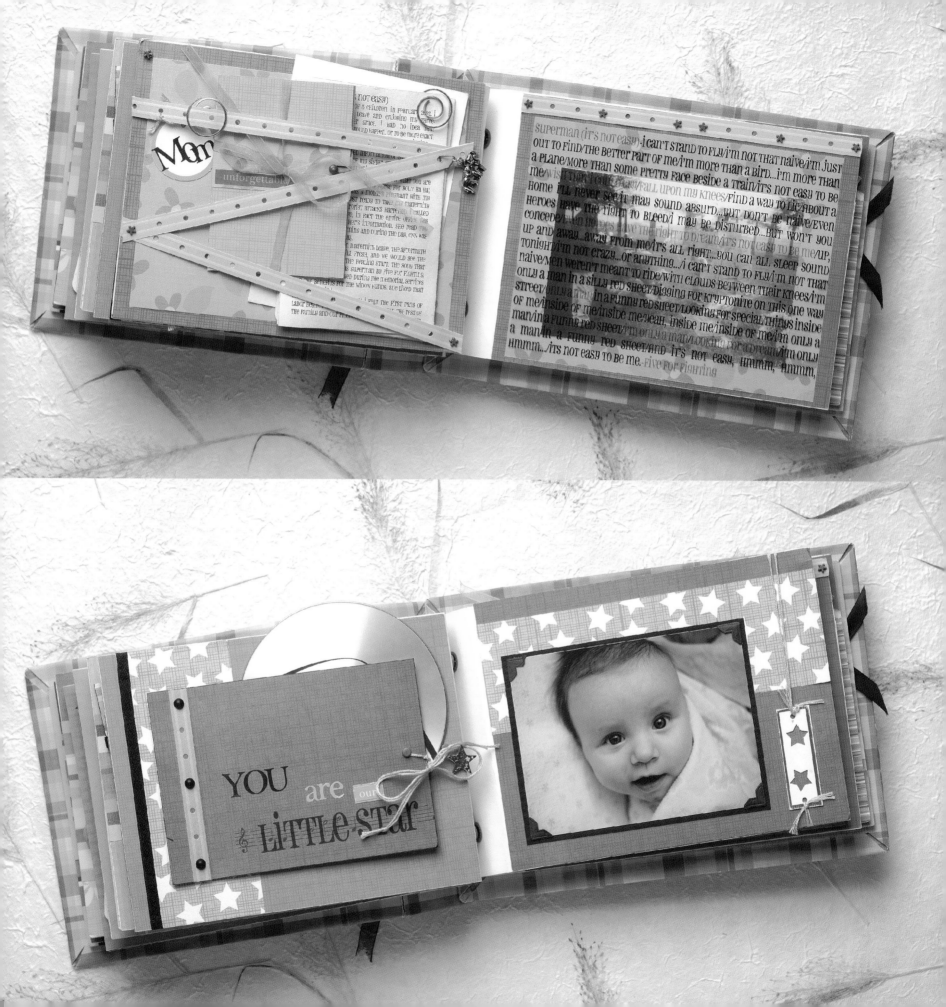

Nia Reddy

And then there were

THREE

A book of a how our family came to be.

NIA · ALVARO · AIDEN

"When love and skill work together, expect a masterpiece." This quote by John Ruskin sums up exactly how I feel about being given the wonderful opportunity to create an album about my family, for they are indeed my masterpiece. My love for my son and my husband, and my passion to create with both my hands and my heart, allowed me to be able to put together a tribute to the both of them.

I began the journey of preserving my family's memories a little over a year ago. I find that each photo I take, and each little note that I scribble down in the journal I carry, is going to be placed in my book of memories, so that my family will know how much they truly mean to me. The importance of creating a place to essentially experience that past, and really see how we lived, laughed, shared, and loved at this point in our lives is the most meaningful treasure I

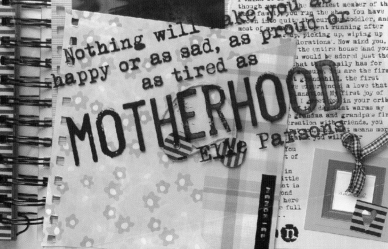

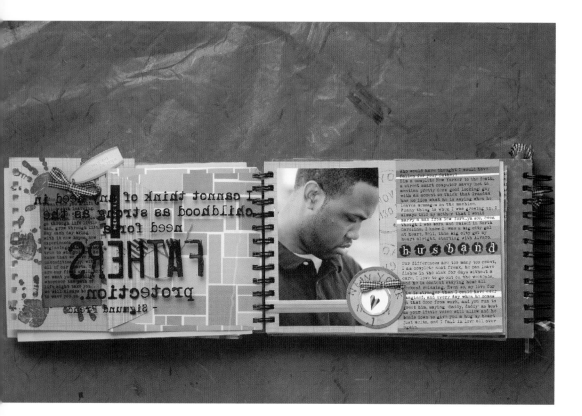

think I could ever give. These are the experiences that I hold in my heart: The way I always walk in my son Aiden's room to find him wearing just one sock in the morning, the way my husband laughs out loud at every little thing on the television, the way Aiden yells "daddy" as soon as Alvaro comes home from work each day, standing on his tiptoes to peek over the metal railing to watch his father come up the stairs–these are the memories that I hold dear. This is why I created this book. This is why it is so meaningful to me.

Meaning can come from the simplest things, and I find that it is those little things that I hold the dearest, and drive me to create. I wanted my son Aiden to have this book to see how his father and I met and how this family began. I wanted him to be able to experience the memories and the stories that we have had these last few years that he is not going to remember, if not for the pages in this album. I want him to know the wishes we have for him, to know how he made us smile, to know that this family of three is the most important thing in my life. I want him to open this album, flip through its pages, read the words and from that have a true understanding of the love that I feel for him and his father–that is what makes this album so meaningful to me, this is why I created it.

John Ruskin could not have said it any better. When love and skill come together, the results are nothing less than extraordinary. My love of my family and my skill as a preserver of memories has resulted in an album that is as near and dear to my heart as those its contents are about- truly my own personal masterpiece.

Every

of

TRULY

MEMORIES

Alone we can do so little

TOGETHER

We can do so much
—HELEN KELLER

neat smart cuddler
loving hilarious talkative fireball

This family is PERFECT.

This album has been a labor of love. Every late night sitting over my scrapping table working on this album has been filled with enjoyment, a few tears, but most of all, lots of love.

As our family grows, I will add to this album, each page representing a new memory in our lives. I cherish each and every page in this book, and each page is a little piece of my heart put on paper. May this family continue to grow, to laugh, to live, to share, and most importantly... to love.

So much fun!

Alvaro, from you I have learned how truly thankful and blessed I can feel being in a loving relationship. I have learned to give my whole heart, to love unconditionally (even when you leave the dishes in the sink without washing them). I have learned the importance of communication, and have allowed myself to really communicate my feelings to you, both good and bad, which is something I used to struggle with. I have learned that I do not always have to go out and spend money to have a good time, that snuggling with you on the couch when Aiden has gone to bed makes me feel better than any five course meal at a fancy restaurant would. I have learned that life is so fulfilling sharing it with a partner. I have learned how to fall in love, over and over again.

ALVARO

Aiden, from you I have learned so many things. First and foremost I have learned how to be patient. I have learned that life is not meant to be rushed and that every single moment should be cherished, and with you, it truly is. I have learned to be a child again, to let my hair down, to play, to rediscover things in new ways and to laugh (luckily you are very good at making me do that). I have learned how to be a mama and even with all the responsibility, all the sleepless nights, all of the runny noses and diaper changes, all of the tantrums (and there are plenty now that you are almost 2 years old) bthis is the gift that I will cherish the most.

AIDEN

what I've learned from you

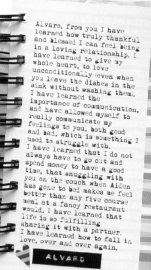

Sandi Minchuck

When I decided to make this album, it initially began for all the wrong reasons: Chatterbox chose to run an album contest that advertised a reward so grand (ten grand to be exact) that I could not refuse to enter. The other thing that caught me was the trip for two to Hawaii. If I won, Jeff and I could finally enjoy a better-late-than-never honeymoon to a wondrous place that I have always longed to visit. So, I set out trying to decide what type of album to make and I realized that I have made albums for most of the members of my family, but had yet to record and document my own life. Then I started to create the pages that would soon fill my album, and I was hooked, not only with the gorgeous papers and innovative embellishments, but on delving into who I thought was me. I no longer had the aspirations of winning, but of creating a book that I could pass on to my children. Hopefully, someday some unborn great-grandchild will find this album hidden away in the attic and discover that I was not perfect and love me more for it.

I decided to name the album 'My Story' which I know is not such an original name or idea for a book about oneself, but that is the point. I *am* an average person. I have an average job. My husband and I live in an average house and drive average cars. It became a release to come home and build this album every night after work; and it became the best form of therapy because the introspection was such a wonderful change of pace. Making it forced me to look into myself and decide the things that were really important, and they are now showcased inside this album. My album will forever hold special meaning in my heart, not only for the obvious reasons, but because I now have an album that tells my story. It is full of hidden journalling and meaning of which only I am aware... Full of pictures that hold special and private places in my heart... Full of meaning and hopes and dreams and things that have changed me for the better. Even more so. it is full of me—an average person with an average life, I've come to realize that I have an extraordinary story to tell, as well as the life I've always wanted.

Why was creating this album so meaningful for me? Good question. To answer it, you have to understand how I started scrapbooking in the first place. My life was basically in turmoil. I had lost my father very suddenly and unexpectedly, six months later my brother died, a few months after that my husband lost his job and I was laid off from my position as a graphic designer. We were the epitome of "Murphy's Law," and I found myself thinking "What now?" I craved an outlet for my overflowing emotions. I set up my studio in our basement and started scrapping. All along my intention was to create a memorial album about the life of my brother, Kevin, and his struggles and accomplishments while living with ALS aka Lou Gehrig's Disease. (ALS is a rapidly progressively fatal neuromuscular disease that attacks the nerve cells that control voluntary muscles. The muscles, unable to move, eventually weaken and die.)

I had years of journaling, newspaper clippings, letters, and memorabilia, but my heart just couldn't begin. Instead I started scrapping everything else. Eventually, my husband got a job, I started freelancing and getting my life back on track, but what began as a way for me to keep sane had turned into a true passion! I was hired at my local scrapbook store and started teaching classes. I was totally hooked on every aspect of this "hobby."

I created dozens of albums over the past three years but the project nearest and dearest to my heart remained a blank slate. Then I saw the ad for the Chatterbox "Make it Meaningful" album contest. The six years that my brother suffered with ALS were the most meaningful in my life. To say he changed my life is an understatement. He also affected everyone he came in contact with, and his legacy will benefit thousands of ALS patients in the years to come. I was with him on the day he was

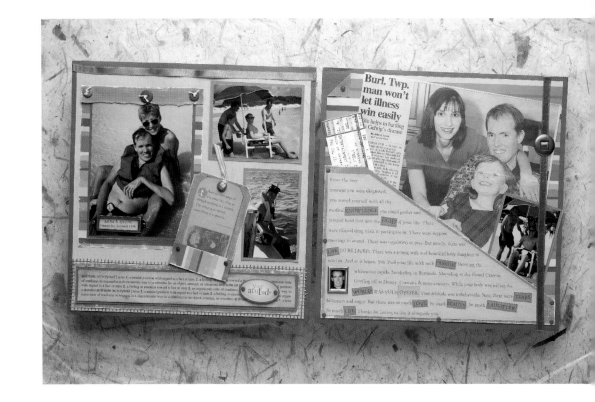

diagnosed, and I held his hand by his bedside six years later when he left us. The moments in between were full of elation and devastation, of uncontrollable laughter and inconsolable tears. But most of all, those years were full of pride, compassion, love and family.

Creating this keepsake was the most difficult, and yet most incredibly rewarding thing I have ever accomplished. To be able to share Kevin's story with thousands of people is an overwhelming privilege, to have a gift for his daughter, my niece Alina, on her wedding day and to have future generations of our family see Kevin as the true hero he was...well, to me that is what makes this entire journey so meaningful.

I called this album, "Through the Eyes of a Hero", because when my brother could no longer speak he began to communicate via the computer. When he could no longer move the mouse to operate the computer, we started to read his lips, and when moving his lips became impossible, we "read" his twinkling Irish eyes.

The Purpose of
life is a life of
Purpose

—Robert Byrne

Krista Fernandez

i Sustain myself with the love of family & friends *maya angelou*

Krista

I am fortunate to be surrounded by so much love from my family and

fernandez

POLAROID
LAND CAMERA   AUTOMATIC 100
DARKEN   LIGHTEN

I am fortunate to be surrounded by wonderful friends and they truly define the person I am. I've been able to take something from each and every one of my friends and use it to make me a better person. I knew that by creating a tribute album to my friends, it would not only be a gift to myself, but a way to say thank you to them for being my friends. When creating this album, I had hoped to capture each of my friends' personalities and their special qualities through the pictures I used and the journaling I wrote. It was important to me to let my loved ones know how blessed I feel to have them in my life.

Creating each layout was a time consuming process. Usually, I am a quick scrapbooker. If something doesn't feel right on a layout, I usually leave it and quickly move on. However, I didn't attach or adhere anything to my Chatterbox layouts until I was 100% sure it fit on the layout.

I also tried to alter the look of everyday embellishments or use out of the ordinary supplies, like vintage lace trim. I hoped that the embellishments, colors, textures and patterns helped represent the person I was scrapbooking. To keep the album consistent, I used some of the same products and handwriting on each of the layouts. Using black and white photos helped with the continuous flow of the album too. Recently, I purchased a new camera, a Canon Rebel SLR and in result, having great photographs in my scrapbooks has become more important to me. I choose to hide all my journaling so the main focus would be on the photographs.

The people I choose to feature in my Friendship album went beyond just friends. I am fortunate to have my mother as one of my dearest friends, as well as my cousin, April. Also, I am lucky to have my boyfriend, Zack, included in my album and consider him my best friend.

Upon completion of my Chatterbox album, I knew I had won. Even if my album was not chosen to be one of the 25 winners, I knew that just by completing the album was enough for me to feel like a winner!

Liz Montoya

What I wish for you...

This album was created at just the right time in my life because I have been in the middle of assessing my own personal hopes and dreams. I want my children to know that being their mommy is and has been the greatest, most fulfilling accomplishment in my life. When my three-year-old told me, "You're the best mommy!" I knew in my heart this is what I was meant to do. I used to measure success and happiness by what a person did or achieved; like whether someone graduated from college or how much money they earned. Fortunately all that has changed. I know firsthand that life doesn't always turn out the way we plan it, but I also know that with God it turns out even better than we can hope for. I also know the most important thing we can give our children is ourself. They need our faith, hopes, and wishes. But above all, they need our love. The words I wrote in this album come from the bottom of my heart. I love my boys dearly and they are my inspiration and joy. The love, hugs, and kisses I receive I cannot put a price on. Their smiles and laughter are rainbows on a cloudy day. I have been blessed with two beautiful souls and I thank God for them every day. He has also entrusted us to give them what they need and defining these needs is where I began to create the album. Someday, I hope this book will be a keepsake that reveals how much I love them. I hope it will be a voice of reason when they have doubts, or a light for direction when they have lost their way.

These thoughts, wishes, and prayers are driven home by my own personal experiences and guided by my faith in God and my conviction that life is precious and we must make the most of all situations—no matter what the circumstances are. As a young girl I also had many hopes and dreams but had to put those dreams on hold. Being the second oldest of seven children, the responsibility of helping my mother and father raise my siblings fell on me. I grew up knowing what it was like not having material things but it taught me to appreciate all the things I do have. It also taught me that the greatest 'things' in my life were my faith, family, and friends. Now when I look at my boys, I know that I have made the right choices, and for doing so, I have achieved more than I could have hoped for. I give thanks to the Lord for these priceless treasures, for the joys and the memories we get to create as a family, and for giving me the freedom to choose which path to follow. I pray my children will do the same. I have reached the point in my life where I can leave behind the questioning, strive to make amends with shortcomings, give thanks for all I have, and leave the rest to God. And knowing this is all we really need.

BeAutIfuL bOy

Paul Christian Montoya

PaUl

You are a GIFT to the
world, a divine work of
art, signed by God.
-Max Lucado

I wish for you to be
happy in whatever
career path you
choose and I pray
that you will put
your faith and trust
in God to lead the
way.

know the plans I
declares the
for you

in your
career

What lies
behind us and
what lies
before us are
tiny matters
compared to
what lies
within us.
-Anonymous

dReAM

For the LORD is good and his
love endures forever; his
faithfulness continues through
all generations. Psalm 100:5

Cousins

The De Leon Family

pray that you will know the
beautiful gift of care and treasured
friendships that grows through the
years and blossoms with both
laughter and tears.

OCT 3 6 2003

Jill Cornelius

When I first decided to enter the Make It Meaningful Contest I knew exactly what my album was going to be about, my cat. For most, this would seem like an unusual choice of subjects, and I was not even sure how to go about doing it. It's easy to do an album about a person because you have their story, their accomplishments, their awards, and their life. But what about a cat? Well, all you have is the cat. I thought that I would dig deeper into the picture of how I could make this album meaningful, and demonstrate to others, not just myself, what my cat means to me.

For most, a cat is a pet. A cat cannot express himself with anything other than purring, meowing or rubbing his head against you. He can't speak any words to offer encouragement, give you a hug, or say "I love you." This album has shown me that all through my pet's life he has given me unconditional love. Making this album has given me the opportunity to see my relationship with Skippy in a different light. I have realized that my cat is more than just a pet; he is a best friend. He was there for me when I was all alone. He has been through the sad and happy times of my life. He is my Hero, because he inspired me to stand up for myself during a period in which I would have just crawled in a hole. I was in an abusive relationship, and all that I had to make me happy was my cat. I would sit and pet him and he would purr, that alone made life perfect. His purr would make me smile, and his happiness was the most important thing in the world to me at that moment.

Skippy is twelve years old now. I know that the end is coming soon and try not to think of it. I know that Skippy will die someday, just like everyone else. Even though he is not my mother or father, my aunt or uncle, he will be missed very much and there will be lots of tears when that day comes. This album

will serve to remind me of him long after he is gone. It will remind me of the times when he ate toast with my daughter when she was a child, how he did silly things like sleep on my head, and how endearing he could be when he would just sit in front of me and meow, wanting to be picked up. It will remind me about how "good" he was when we brought each of the other cats home, and how he made them and everyone else welcome in our home.

Without entering this contest I wouldn't have been given the chance to show myself and everyone else what a truly special part of my life my cat is. For that I thank you. Because you have give me the strength to sit down and write my story, one that brings tears to my eyes and joy to my heart, all brought on by a little orange ball of fur that I call Skippy.

Kandice Matzler

what makes me tick...

Cathartic- adj 1: emotionally purging

The word "cathartic" perfectly describes my experience in making this scrapbook album. It turned into
a complete journey of self-discovery and a surprise
emotional cleansing! I quickly realized that in the
countless hours of my time scrapbooking, I have
never expressed on paper anything real about me.
Hundreds of events and fond memories have been
carefully documented, but never actual emotions or
relationships that mean something. The entire
album proved to be a challenge. I knew that for it to
have any meaning at all, it would have to be raw, and
vulnerable, and completely honest... and honesty is
intimidating, especially when it's being preserved for
future generations!

Before I could even start one single page, I decided
to completely analyze myself and break down every
aspect of my life into exactly what it was and why it
was there. I needed to pinpoint my favorite memories, my motives, my desires, my disappointments,
and even my purpose in life to recognize which
chapters of "My Story" should be told. So I
mapped out my life— people, places, friends, inter-
ests, goals and heartbreaks... everything. To be honest, it was emotionally draining. I struggled to find
the right words to give justice to my emotions, and
this experience forced me to sort through it. I was
able to distinguish the people and events that have
molded me and impacted who I am, and it was so
liberating! I have been given a renewed sense of
gratitude for those that I love and appreciation of the
extraordinary blessings in my life. It is also an
encouragement to reflect on moments that were a
struggle at the time, but now I realize they have
made me stronger.

Even difficult times have strengthened my faith and made my spirit more resilient. I can see that time after time God has provided for me, when I didn't understand, and that inspires me for what lies ahead.

Another way of describing my experience in creating this album is therapeutic. Having the opportunity to see every aspect of my life stripped down to the basics has given me a new perspective. It has helped me accept my past, recognize what really matters, and be thankful for what I have that could easily be forgotten. I can also see the mistakes I have made, and how they have made me stronger. Being able to come to terms with every aspect of my life at this point makes an uncertain future less frightening, and it energizes me to see where the next road leads. Documenting who I am right now has challenged me to identify who I want to be in five, ten, or twenty years... and it reminds me to appreciate all that I will experience and learn along the way.

Nicole Keller

Pieces of the Past

Album Completed
November 2003

During the Summer of 2002 I sat down with my last living grandparent, Imogene Funk. I wanted to listen as she related stories from her past before the memories were lost to time. She told stories of her children, her parents, and her grandparents. Some of the memories were good, and some of them were unpleasant. Whether the memories are cheerful or not, we can relate to the struggles of those who went before us and learn from their mistakes. Most of all we can see that people are the same today as they were in the past and discover how the more things change the more they really do stay the same.

Little did I know that these would be my last deep conversations with Grandmummy. I saw her again at Christmas and by the next Summer she was gone. I am so thankful that I was given the opportunity to gather pieces of the past.

- Nicole Keller

Like the end of another season,
So the circle of life continues.
A new generation blooms,
And the old fades away.
A new season comes around
And the old sleeps.
Rejoice in the new
And mourn with a joyful
heart the old,
But always remember.

When I first began to create this album my intention was to have a place to record stories from my past. My family has always been precious to me and understanding my roots has helped to provide me with a true sense of self. My mom had presented me with photos of relatives from her side of the family and I knew the names of the faces in the photos and our familial relationships, but in reality I knew very little about the people in the pictures.

During the summer of 2002, in a providential sense of timing, I sat down with my grandmother and showed her the pictures my mom had given to me and asked her to tell me things that she remembered about her parents and grandparents. For a few hours she reminisced while I listened and tape-recorded the conversation. Some of the stories were humorous, and others were shocking, sad, or warm and fuzzy. The stories remained on audio tapes stashed in a dresser drawer as I waited for the opportunity to compile them with the photographs into an album. I had mistakenly believed that I had many more years with my grandmother and time was of no concern.

In June of 2003, I checked my email and was shocked to see a note from my mom. Her email stated that my Grandmother had suddenly become ill, and if I wanted to see her I needed to come home quickly. That afternoon I boarded a plane and flew from Texas to Pennsylvania. Many other family members also arrived to be with the matriarch of our family during the last days of her life. We kept a vigil in her hospital room and surrounded her with our love as she passed.

Before we returned to our respective homes my sisters and I climbed the ladder into my grandmother's attic and searched through a lifetime of mementos. My grandmother was not rich but the treasures in the attic were priceless. We found old Christmas cards, diaries, autograph books, and letters from old boyfriends. We unearthed old ID cards, photos, and postcards from penpals. Each of us selected a few special items to keep.

When I decided to enter the Chatterbox contest I intended to seize the opportunity to pull together the photos, the stories, and the memorabilia to create a heritage album. I wanted the album to go beyond the birth dates, death dates, and marriage statistics of my ancestors and help to bring them to life by telling the stories behind the pictures. However, as the album began to take shape, the project became even more meaningful to me. As I transcribed the stories onto paper and studied the photos and memorabilia, I learned more about my ancestors and myself than I ever thought I would. I learned about the parts of their environment that shaped their lives and formed them into the spirited individuals that they were. I discovered how families struggled together through hard times and made decisions that would change the directions of their lives, their childrens' lives, and my life. Most importantly I learned more of the reasons behind why I am who I am and the meaningfulness of the pieces of my past.

Catherine Maud Flora Brown
Mother to Vera
Grandmother to Imogene
Great Grandmother to Jane
Great Great Grandmother to Nicole

Catherine M. Brown

Catherine Maud Flora Brown and Benjamin Franklin Brown were Gram's (Vera Jane Brown Snowden's) parents. Catherine was called "Grammy" by her grandchildren. Grandmummy remembers her grandmother to a perfectionist who wanted to live in the best end of town. She came to Chambersburg from Dry Run to work as a farm hand for her sister Benjamin Franklin Brown also came to work on the farm from Strasburg, PA and helped to take care of the horses and cows. They met there and eventually got married.

He built a duplex on Scotland Avenue because Grammy really wanted a house. They helped to take care of Imy and Peep and their cousins Jean and Aubrey when their parents could not.

August 18, 1953

Resolutions on the death of our Dear brother John B. Wagner on July 28, 1953, were offered, and then adopted as read: Viz:

Whereas in the allwise providence of God, Brother John B. Wagner, our kind, very willing worker and loyal class member, has been called to his eternal home: and

Whereas, by his death there has been taken from us, one who was a devoted Christian and profound interest in all the activities of the Men's Bible Class, Sunday School and of the church: and

Whereas, We, as members of the Men's Bible Class feel the deepness of the loss we have sustained.   Therefore, be it resolved:

First:- That we the members of the class express our appreciation of his Christian character, his personal consecration to Christ, and to the Church, his loyalty to this class and to the entire school, his faithfulness to every duty, and his zeal for the furtherance of Christ's Kingdom.

Second:-That we are grateful to almighty God for this life that has been lived among us and earnestly pray that his influence and spirit may long abide within our hearts.

Third:- That a copy of these resolutions be spread upon our minutes and a copy be sent by our secretary to the bereaved family.

Frank W. McElroy
Frank W. McElroy

Fred E. Strickler
Fred E. Strickler
COMMITTEE.

The Death of Ben

Ben worked as an electrician at Letterkenney. Because he was blind in one eye, he had difficulty judging distances. On July 28, 1953 he was working on a pole when he touched a live wire. When Ben was electrocuted they tried to resuscitate him for hours. Grandmummy was at a Sunday School picnic, and when she got home, Gram said, "Ben's been killed."

Grandmummy didn't believe her and thought, "He's too good to die." She went upstairs and got down on her knees and prayed about it. She thought he might need insulin (he was diabetic) and called the doctor. They went to see him and finally the hospital staff gave up resuscitation efforts and sent him to the funeral home. Grandmummy remembers that there were so many people at the viewing. Ben was only 53 and the twins (Mom) were 11.

LKY EMPLOYE ELECTROCUTED ON LIGHT POLE

John B. Wagner Killed In Contact With Wire At Nearby Depot

CORONER IMPANELS JURY FOR INQUIRY

LKY EMPLOYE ELECTROCUTED ON LIGHT POLE

(Continued from page one)

Ben's Glasses

Considering how much I love scrapbooking, I might never have starting doing it if it weren't for my son. When I took my first class, I learned (as most every scrapper does) all about preserving photographs and preserving memories through journaling. And, as many scrappers do, as I progressed I fell under the spell of the artistry of the pages, and while I still tried to tell my stories in my scrapbooks, I wasn't always as thorough and true to those memories as I should have been. It was time to find a balance between representing myself artistically and keeping the past alive.

I mentioned before that if it weren't for my little boy, I might never have started scrapbooking. I started writing letters to my son before he was even born. This was way before I even knew what scrapbooking was, and little did I know that one day I would look back on those letters and be reminded that no matter what happens, good or bad, there is a story that needs to be told. When my little boy was born with a rare genetic syndrome, my desire to write down my thoughts and feelings became even more important as a way of coping with the every hour, every day stresses and triumphs of having a special child.

I went to my first scrapbooking class and found an outlet that I really enjoyed. I started making books of my son's milestones and accomplishments, and it became a real creative outlet for me. But in all of that, I found it difficult to scrap the trials we were going through.

If I were asked, "what did making this album mean to you?" I would have to say that it was a challenge from beginning to end. Not only did making it put my creativity to the test, it also challenged me to tell

things like they really are, and not put on those "rosy glasses" all the time in my storytelling. Making this album enabled me to bring my scrapbooking to a more human and intimate level, and share the story of a little boy who is truly a remarkable person in spite of everything he has been through.

I learned a lot from this experience. As I was putting the pages together for the album, I read and reread all the letters I wrote, and realized that if I had not kept these memories just as they were originally written, I wouldn't appreciate where my son and family are now in our lives, and how we got here. It is really easy to forget over time, and that is why a project like this is so important. Making this album means that never again will I "skimp" on my memories, good or bad, that I put into one of my scrapbooks.

I long to accomplish a great and noble task, but it is my chief duty to accomplish small tasks as if they were great and noble.

-Helen Keller

Adrienne Looman

Timeless
memories

When you think of a memory, it usually
involves people, or places that were
significant in your life at that time.
The most wonderful part of memories
is that you don't need a camera to
remember them. But as time passes,
little particles of that memory begin
to fade... and what is left is a mere
fraction of it. This is why I have
gathered my most precious memories
and combined them as one in this album.
These are my Timeless Memories.

For many years I have wanted to make an album such as the one I entered into this contest. I have made many albums to date, but this one is very unique. It's not sorted by the same year, or memories of one person, or one occasion. Instead I looked back at all my years of memories, and chose my most precious photos. Some of these represent a period in my life which was sheer happiness...others are ground breaking.

One of my favorite parts of making this album was the title page. The name was "Timeless Memories." I had so much fun sitting down and explaining what a timeless memory meant to me. I also added a watch crystal containing watch particles to represent "time captured," which is what we do when we scrap our memories. The page reads:

"When you think of a memory, it usually involves people, or places that were significant in your life at that time. The most wonderful part of memories is that you don't need a camera to remember them. But as time passes, little particles of that memory begin to fade…and what is left is a mere fraction of it. This is why I have gathered my most precious memories and combined them as one in this album. These are my timeless memories."

I can honestly say that I look at my layouts and journaling in a whole new way. I often find myself debating a change in a layout to make sure it is more meaningful to me, and our family. Though scrapbooking is a creative outlet for us to use our imagination and creativity, there's a deeper meaning to our hard work that future generations will greatly appreciate.

As a comfort to my sister, I began sending scrap-books to her so she could be a part of my families' life during the distance that separates us. I soon found that I also have been comforted in being able to share the day-to-day activities with her. We wouldn't want to miss a moment of life's exciting memories even though we are not together.

When I started our sisters' album, it was a way to once again provide comfort to her as her hopes of moving back to Ohio were shattered. At the time we were creating our album, I did not realize the impact it would have on myself. I always knew my sister was my friend, my inspiration, and my confidant. There is no other person in this world that under-stands me the way she does. What I didn't know was how much of what I am feeling she is feeling too. During our hours on the phone, we had never discussed these deep feelings we have for each other. When I finally read our completed album, with my box of tissues in hand, I became awed at how alike we are; realizing what a true friend she is and how much our relationship and bond has grown as adults. What I now feel for our friendship overwhelms me with pride, love, and admiration.

As I show our album to friends and family, I am shown the true meaning. A close friend read the album, with tears in her eyes, and told me how she wished she had a sister to share her life with like I do. I will always remember her feelings of envy at our relationship. Her reaction to the album made me realize how fortunate I am to have my sister. Everyone should be given the opportunity to share in such a unique friendship (if they could be 'just like us', how lucky they would be). The thoughts and feelings within our album will be in my heart forever. It is that which will help me through the miles that separate us. Oh, how lucky I am to have her.

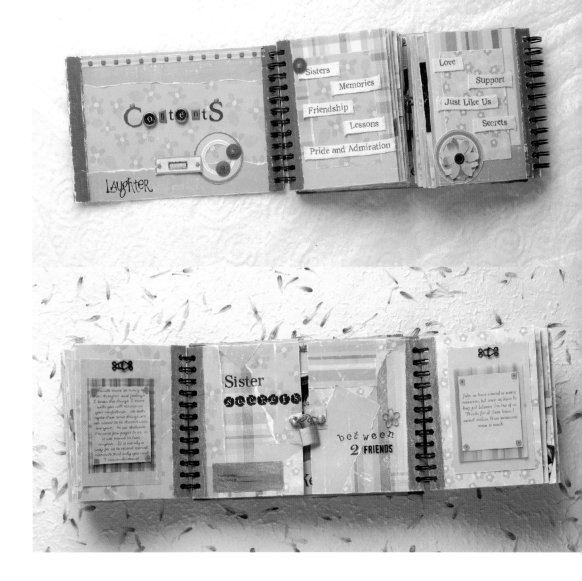

My sister and I shared so much throughout the journey of this album. It only seems right that she take part in sharing her reflections on what the album now means to her.

This scrapbook was started to share feelings, thoughts, and memories between Julie and I. I believe we accomplished that goal. Although throughout this journey I have come to find a new meaning in this book, Now, I read this scrapbook and find feelings that were not always stated or expressed between us. We each wrote our own thoughts while separated, yet discovered how much we are alike and how we feel so many things the same way. The true heartfelt feelings that were expressed are words to some, but true appreciation to me. This book holds such a special meaning because we are sharing those thoughts and feelings that are so easily overlooked. To read what Julie shared and expressed takes our friendship to the next level.

The scrapbook Julie and I created shares a special relationship between two sisters, two friends. During our separation, Julie in Ohio and me in Texas, we have come to find comfort in sharing our passions. We talk for hours on the phone and share missed moments through our scrapbooks. This scrapbook was just another way for us to share our passions, but it really gave us a gift, the gift of memories, thoughts, and friendship.

Scrapbooks are made to share memories with family and friends. The contents of this book also brought me to understand a friendship between sisters that we have been lucky enough to share.

Lara Stern

the Romsos Sisters

Natalie: 4 yrs.
Lara: 2 ½ yrs.
Lisa: 3 ½ mo.

Hawaii
May 10
1978

SISTERS share the...
MEMORIES of yesterday
The JOYS of today
and
The HOPE of tomorrow.

The Romsos sisters have created wonderful memories together: family vacations at the farm, building forts, boogie boarding, snow ice cream, weddings, and now babies! We have also created memories that we wish we could file away forever: changing grades on reports cards, tickle torture, fingernail fights, and not walking to school with each other. However, as we reminisced, laughed and cried through stacks of photos, we realized that the simple day-to-day memories are the ones that matter most. In many ways, these simple memories still define who we are today - Princess Lisa and her "babies," Green Thumb Lara the commentator and Drill Sergeant, Natalie and her craft box. Raising three girls with such different personalities, there were moments when our mom prayed that one day we would not only love, but also like each other.

As we created this album we found a much deeper appreciation and understanding for each other and who we were growing up. We found that each of us has been blessed with different strengths and skills to help make each page special. We found that even though we still have very different personalities, we are more alike than we thought. We found our parents had great insight on raising three girls and what makes each of us unique. (Thanks mom and dad for your help!) We found that words and pictures take on a greater significance than we could have ever realized on our own. We have found that mom's prayers were answered. We love and like each other more than we could have ever dreamed! These pages just begin to tell the story of the Romsos sisters. We look forward to adding more memories in the future.

Renee Foss

to Olivia, Sam + Harry

Love, Mommy

KiSS tHe MooN

My grandmother passed away suddenly fifteen years ago from a heart attack, and ever since there has been a hole in my heart. My parents divorced when I was two, and my mom and I lived with my granny for several years before my mother remarried. My granny was my caretaker during that time, and, in her own special way, has imprinted herself on my life and values. My granny was (to me) the most sophisticated, put-together, intelligent woman I knew. I always wanted to be like her, to grow up and exude one tenth of the class she did. She was my advisor, confidant, and shoulder to cry on. She accepted me for who I was, and what I did (whether she approved or not). Of course, when she didn't approve I had to endure a good 'discussion' or two on the matter, but she always did so in such a loving, caring, and respectful manner. I never resented her, never questioned her advice.

My grandmother has shaped the woman I have become, even more so than my mother has. Not a day goes by where she isn't in my heart and my thoughts. Every time I follow one of her 'codes' to life, she is there. Every time I can carry myself with dignity in the face of adversity, she is there. Every time I am frustrated with life, she is there. I wanted to create a tribute album to her for some time but never knew how or where to start. I don't know much about her childhood or early life — I never had the chance to ask her. I finally decided to honor her by documenting what I have learned from her, both directly and indirectly. Some of it is serious, some is silly, but that's how life should be. I want my family to know why my grandmother is so important to me and why sometimes I speak of her with a smile on my face, and other times with tears in my eyes.

I feel that my album expresses my love and admiration for my grandmother in such a manner, and that is what makes it meaningful for me. I wanted to be true to myself, which in itself honors the way my grandmother conducted her life. The elements in the album are chosen to represent some aspect of her life. Nothing is random. When the album was finished and I looked at it in its entirety I knew she would have been pleased.

Becky Fleck

Josh Billings once said, "A dog is the only thing on earth that loves you more than he loves himself." No truer words were ever spoken. When we adopted Jackson and Hannah, our two yellow labs, it was the first time we'd had dogs. Naturally, I took an obscene amount of photos, as though they were my first-born children. As it turns out, all of my children have four legs, much to my mother's dismay!

I've always dreamed of writing a children's book. It was number six on my "Top Ten Things I Want To Do Before I Die" list. (I must confess that to date, I've only accomplished three of those ten things!) As I got to know our puppies, I began to contemplate a children's story about their lives, told from their perspective. Jackson and Hannah's hilarious antics, clumsy, but occasionally graceful frolics, and lively, unique personalities were the foundation of the story. The photos I had amassed were the icing on the cake.

As I began to organize this scrapbook, every photo I came across of Jackson and Hannah conjured up a wonderful memory. The book took off, and before I knew it, I had written a children's story. As I looked over my photos, I realized that most of them were taken outside. The Reading Room, Den and Rec Room papers were the perfect choice for the book. I hit my local scrapbook store and gathered my supplies (paying their electric bill for the month in the process!), and was off and cropping.

Honest to gosh, this book was so much fun to crop! I laughed out loud many times, remembering why Jackson had a goofy look on his face or why Hannah was in the snit she was in. My husband will tell you of the numerous times I would whine to him, "I wa-a-ant ano-o-other pu-u-uppy" every time I would look at a photo of them when they were little. (His gentle reminder of potty training silenced me immediately.) Jackson and Hannah are filled with such joy and delight, and I felt I was able to convey their essence in this scrapbook.

Amber (Horsely) Wooten

my story

Am I strong enough?

A Life Changing Experience

As I have learned and progressed page by page, scrapbooking has become more of a passion than a hobby. It is not just about finding the best paper and the perfect layout for a great picture…it is about recording the precious moments of one's life in a way that can take you once again to that place in time. It is about touching all the senses, especially the heart.

When the opportunity came to enter the Chatterbox contest, my goal was to do just that…touch someone's heart. At the time, my mother was going through the challenges of breast cancer and I was amazed every day at her strength and positive attitude. I knew that sharing her story would be a chance for me and others to learn something special, possibly even life changing. Recording her journey through pictures and thoughts has created a treasure that will be handed down through the generations of family and friends. Each page will show and tell her story in a bright, colorful, and creative way…just as she sees and lives her life.

My life has truly been touched while creating this album. As I have watched my mother go through this experience, I have learned what life is really about. It's about making every moment count, living and loving unconditionally, because as cliché as it may sound, we never know when what we have might be taken away from us. It can happen so quickly and without warning. Everyday is a gift and each day that she lives, my mother touches and at times, changes lives. I know that she has changed mine. This book is dedicated to my mother, for everything she is and all that she has become.

I am happy to say that there is not yet an end to this story. I continue to write each day on a fresh, clean page...open to whatever words and thoughts my cherished life enfolds.

Recently, a lady standing in line just before me at the store, turned and said to me, "You are a beautiful bald woman". Who would have thought that those words could feel like such a compliment but they did. Then she said to me, "And there is something in your eyes and just the way you carry yourself...". I'm sure she had no idea how much she was really saying to me and how much it meant to my tender spirit. I believe that we are truly strengthened and measured during the times of our individual adversities. I would sincerely hope that when my story does come to an end, that through this challenge... this life experience, through the fears and concerns... I have stood tall and kept hope's brightness in my eyes.

Not yet the end.
October 28, 2003

Vicki Harvey

Lucile Larson was a very special woman and I consider myself very blessed to have been her granddaughter. She taught me many valuable things and I am eternally grateful to her for that

Grandma swinging at the school in Malden Rock, WI. Early 1980's

MEmoRiEs

of Grandma Larson

It's been eleven years since my grandmother passed away and yet I still miss her terribly. It saddens me that she would never get to meet my children, and makes me even sadder that they would never have the chance to know her. I just know she would have loved them and they certainly would have loved her. It makes me happy to be able to share a bit of her with them in the pages of this book.

She was a very kind and gentle woman and at the same time strong and independent. Upon recent examination of my own life I realized that she has been quite an influence on who I have become. She taught me practical skills as well as character building life skills. I have admired and respected her strength and independence throughout my life. I wanted to emulate her and I hope I have made her proud. Her kind nature and strong character are qualities that I always want to carry with me down the path of my life.

It puts a smile on my face when little things remind me of her. When she passed away I inherited a few of her belongings. My pajamas now lie neatly folded in the drawer of a dresser that was hers. I often wonder what she kept in there. As a child I would sit for hours sorting through the treasures in her old wooden sewing box. I loved looking at the wooden thimbles, cards of antique buttons, and pearl-headed pins. The box now sits on the mantle of my fireplace. Just the scent when I open it can transport me back to when I was a little girl watching her sew. I used bits and pieces of the notions from that box on the pages of my album.

As I've grown older I've become quite interested in family history and stories of the past. Unfortunately,

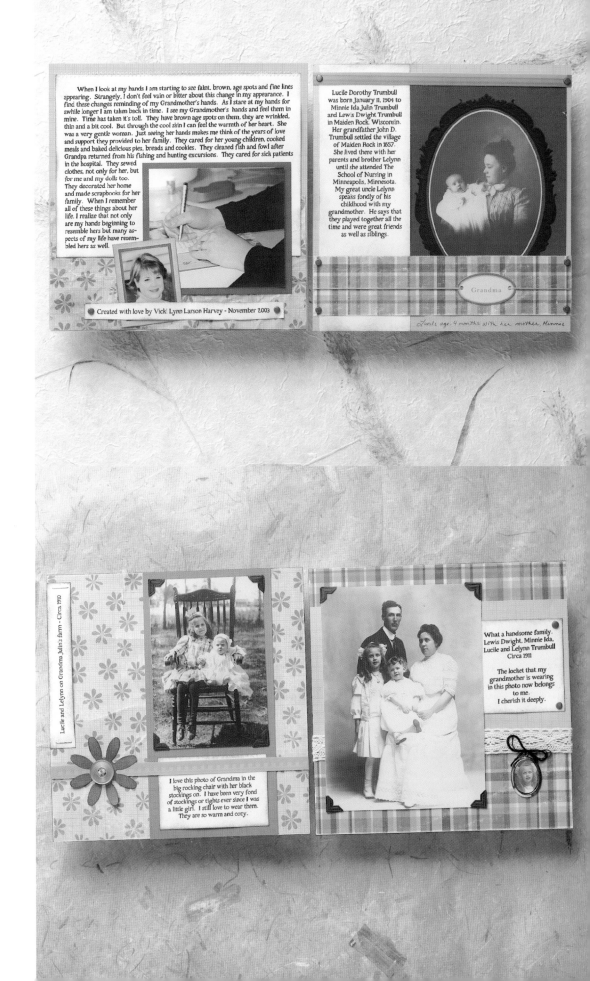

When Lucile graduated from high school she attended River Falls Normal School. She obtained her teaching certificate in 1924 and taught grammar school for a couple of years.
When I was in the third grade I can remember wanting to be a teacher like my grandma. I wanted to be an art teacher.

Lucile Dorothy Trumbull
her high school graduation photo
Circa 1922

Grandma, me and my dad, Dwight. May 1985 - My high school graduation party

this interest didn't peak until after my grandmother passed away. I am blessed, however, to have a small window of insight into my grandma's past through her brother, my great-uncle Lelynn. I recently discovered his love of family history. He is 94 years old and has a memory that is even better than mine. While I was visiting him one day he showed me genealogical family history dating back to the 1600's complete with photographs. I was fascinated as we sat for hours and he related the tales behind the photos of my grandma. Many of the stories I had never heard before. He has been a wealth of knowledge. I knew I had to get these stories recorded on paper for my children and future generations before they were lost completely.

I was so excited about the finished album that I had to show it to my family right away. Many of them were so touched that they cried tears of joy and remembrance. The album opened the door to even more dialogue and memories. To me that is what scrapbooking is truly all about.

Lucile
Circa 1930

Mom, Dad and I at my pinning ceremony
May 1989

For reasons I am unsure of, my grandma decided to quit teaching and become a nurse. She attended The School of Nursing at Northwestern Hospital in Minneapolis, Minnesota. She left nurse's training without graduating for an intended marriage. She moved back to Maiden Rock and started to prepare for her upcoming wedding. Sadly, she never heard from Harold, the gentleman she was to marry, after she moved. The reasons for the lost communication are still unknown. Somehow she found out that a physician in Cokato, Minnesota was looking for a nurse for his office. She contacted him and he offered her the job. She moved to Cokato and began working there.
I began my college career in the fall of 1985. My initial plan was to be a physician. I changed my major to nursing at the end of my freshman year. I decided that I really wanted to have time to raise a family like my grandmother did. I graduated in May of 1989 with a BA in Nursing from Gustavus Adolphus College.

Grandpa
party inc
his wife E
am not su
niece as t
sure of

After Lucile had been living and working in Cokato for awhile
she met Alfred Larson. They were married September 1, 1935
in Maiden Rock. They lived in Cokato and raised their two
children there. Their first child was a girl, Vernita born
October 25, 1936. Their second child was born September 16,
1941. It was a boy, my father, Dwight Julin Larson.

As a little girl I loved looking at Grandma's wedding photos.
She wore a cathedral length veil and I remember thinking how
beautiful and classic she looked. I wanted to have that same
look when I got married so I made a veil that was fashioned
after hers. During the planning of my wedding she spoke
often of how excited she was to attend and was on a quest for
a new dress to wear to the ceremony. Unfortunately, she
passed away on May 12, 1992, five months before my
wedding. On my wedding day my "something old" was a lace
handkerchief that belonged to her. It was very special to me.

The thing I remember most about my grandmother was her creativity.
She sewed many of her clothes, clothes for me and my sister and
clothes for our dolls. My father built a dollhouse for me for Christmas
one year. My Christmas gift from my grandmother that year was a
full set of curtains for the windows in the dollhouse. I still have the
dollhouse and the curtains are still hanging. She also sewed many of
the curtains, tablecloths, and furniture covers in her home. I have made
all of the window treatments in my home thanks to her influence.
Sewing was my passion before I discovered scrapbooking. She was a
very handy woman as well. If she needed a shelf to display items in
her home she would build one. She also enjoyed painting and was quite
talented. I remember the cute decorations that she painted on her
kitchen cupboards. Speaking of her kitchen, I will never forget the
wonderful aroma that came from that room every time we visited.
She was an amazing cook. I still have many of her recipes and use them
often. When my sister and I would spend time at her house she would
always have some type of craft or project for us to do. I especially
remember the scrapbooks she would have us work on. We would cut
pictures out of old magazines and catalogs and paste them into
homemade books. I loved gardening and had a plethora of seed
catalogs. I loved all of the colors in the seed catalogs and would
inevitably cut my pictures from those catalogs. Every time I get a
seed catalog in the mail I think fondly of those times with her. That
early cutting and pasting was my first experience with scrapbooking.
All through my growing up years I kept a scrapbook with photos and
newspaper and magazine clippings. I know now that I was greatly
influenced by my grandmother to do that. That was the beginning of
my scrapbooking obsession. I now scrapbook archivally and wish that
she could she the work that I do now.

Corinne French

Going through my pictures brought a flood of wonderful memories that made the creation of the album so very rewarding. This album was extremely meaningful because I am consumed with scrapbooking and this was the first project dedicated to "My Story." I tell others that they have a story worth telling and not to hold back on their journaling and yet, I often do not really document things appropriately myself. I have always had the desire to tell "My Story," but it never became a priority. The "Make it Meaningful" contest provided me with just motivation that I needed and the beautiful products went perfectly with every detail of my story! (Everything fit so well together - it was as if those papers and scrapbook love words were created just for me!) I set out to create an album that would help me remember my childhood as well as all of the people and events that, I believe, helped shape my character. Also, I wanted my boys to know how much I love life and still do... I did not want there to be any doubt of the kind of woman that I am or of the woman I want to become. They already know my faults. I wanted them to see me in a different light.

I have loved paper crafts since I was a small child. My dad's famous line was, " If you could get an "A" in scrapbooking, you'd be VALEDVICTORIAN!" While I may not be able to attain grades for my scrapbooking, this book seemed to be a coming together of all my scrapbooking abilities as well as my fond memories of childhood and great hopes for the future. By creating this book, I was able to accomplish the scrapbooking goal of telling "My Story." Raising small children is like re-roofing a house each and every day and often not feeling a sense of completion. Telling my story on such wonderfully coordinated papers was a huge sense of accomplishment. It provided me with source of loveliness that my soul craves.

Creating this book also had a deeper sense of significance. It made me evaluate where I have been, who I am becoming, and where I want to go.

"I dwell in possibility"

This quote by, Emily Dickinson perfectly describes me. Today, I feel like I too have learned to dwell in the possibility of what lies ahead. I love this life that I have been given and I hope my children will always be able to see that in me. This book served as wings to all of my hopes, dreams, and goals for the future!

Beth Pettry

I have been lucky enough to receive two throwaway cameras from my husband while he has been stationed in Iraq. Miraculously, the photos were astounding. They portrayed many different aspects of what our soldiers go through each day, and I could see my husband's personality shining through in each shot.

Some people think making an album or a scrapbook page about someone you dearly love is easy, but in all actuality it is very difficult. You become emotionally attached to the work. You want it to represent everything that individual means to you. As I created this book, a great deal of emotions flowed through me. Pride, honor, loneliness, fear, sorrow, devotion, love, and anger are just some of the things I felt in my heart. As I dove diligently into my work, I knew that not only did I want to represent my husband, but I also wanted the book to parallel the environment that he is currently in. When individuals pick up the book, I first want them to see the worn, tattered appearance, because that is how our men and women in uniform feel who are stationed in Iraq. Then, and most importantly, I wanted them to focus on John through the photos and my journaling. I tried to carefully select photos that best fit the Chatterbox Journaling Tile headers, so as the viewers saw the pictures they would also have journaling that supported the photos on each page.

My husband, a loving and funny man, is not one to disclose his emotions. He keeps them bottled up inside, and I have to read his physical behaviors to know what he is going through. John, striving for me to understand through the barrier of distance, has slightly changed how he releases his emotions. I find that he just throws them into emails or random phone conversations, because he so badly needs me to understand. The day after I finished my album he wrote me a brief message on email. Buried within the hub-bub of his everyday "how's things going" questions, he made this statement, " I never thought I'd ever kneel over and watch my best friend take his last breath." And as soon as I read those lines I knew, not only was I proud that I had created this album for my husband but I was also proud that I honored his fallen friend within its pages, too.

When I first heard of the Chatterbox contest, I was so excited! Two months and three attempts at an album later, I found myself frustrated, and thought about not entering. I started with amazing portraits of my beautiful daughter, and though the pages were filled with beauty, I felt like my journaling was becoming very generic. You know those photos that don't have a story, so you have to make something up. I do love my daughter, but I have written the same thing over and over in her albums. It seems that in trying to create the most beautiful layout, we forget that the quality or beauty of the photo is not most important. Many photos from our childhood never get scrapped because they are not high quality. Generic words that are made up to match a picture that has no story are not meaningful. I wanted to express feelings and memories in my heart, not just some words that would sound nice. Most of all, I wanted to give my daughter memories of someone besides herself.

After watching my daughter with her grandmother one day, I became inspired. As she played and cuddled with my mother, I reminisced about the moments spent with each of my grandparents and the beautiful attributes that each of them had. I had finally found my subject for the contest! I wanted to share with my daughter the beautiful memories of the relationships that I had shared with my grandparents. I wanted her to know who her grandparents are/were and understand that she is a part of them. Finally, I understood what "Make It Meaningful" was about. Finally, I was finally able to work comfortably on the album, and everything just seemed to come together.

I enjoyed reminiscing about all of the wonderful times I had spent with each grandparent. I even thought about my great grandmother and the sign above her sink that read "If Mom Says No, Ask

Grandma." I thought about very special things that I hadn't spoken of for years. I have been so tied up with my busy life that I realized my daughter might never know these people as I had, and I might never share the stories that needed to be shared. And even though each story wasn't the most touching or emotional, I shared with her the truth. It is easy to make up beautiful words about someone, but to me, it was much more beautiful to share the honest things that I remembered, even if they were miniscule.

What had begun as a contest had turned into an emotional journey. I hope my daughter will treasure the things in this book as much as I do, and I hope she will someday add myself and my husband to the book, and pass it to her children with love. Thank you to Chatterbox for motivating me, and thank you to each of my grandparents, and their love for inspiring me.

Shannon & Dino Watt

Four years ago my father died unexpectedly. I was 8 months pregnant with my second child, and coping with his loss was difficult. What made it even more painful was that I have only my memories, and a handful of photos to pass on to my own children. This experience transformed the way I create my scrapbooks. The stories became more important than the trendy techniques and the perfect photo shoots. It became my journal, a living history for my children and their posterity. I wanted the comfort of knowing that if anything were ever to happen to me, my kids would have a tangible piece of me with them always.

This album is incredibly meaningful to us for many reasons. First, I think it's a great love story, and a fun read! But more importantly, it's an ongoing gift for our family. I hope that while my kids grow up they will flip through the pages and feel the love we have for each other, and in turn, for them. I want this album to be an example of what true love is, and how to find someone who compliments them the way we do for each other. I want my kids to see that we were young once, and we know exactly what they will be going through- that we really can relate to them!

Lastly, I think this album is a special gift Dino and I gave ourselves. I foresee a new anniversary tradition of snuggling up on the couch, thumbing through our album, and reflecting on what great blessings we have. When we are going through rough times, we have an incredible reminder of why we are together. It was wonderful to create an album celebrating something positive, wholesome, and good: an old-fashioned love story.

Men in their generations are like leaves of the trees. The wind blows and one year's leaves are scattered on the ground; but the trees burst into bud and put on fresh ones when the spring comes round.

-Homer

Anna Armendariz

On a recent trip to New Jersey, I visited a farmhouse built in the 1800's. Nestled in a secluded lot of trees, it exists peacefully. The floors creak, fireplaces crackle, and walls beg to be touched. This quiet, unassuming home beckoned to me. I imagined births, deaths, love, laughter, and heartache all bonded into the very framework and structure of such a home.

My life is quiet...unassuming. Looking at me, what do you see? Certainly not a completely secure person. I rarely focus on myself and my life. It often ends up in disarray as a result. Creating an album about me is harder than it may seem. I was forced in front of the unforgiving lens of the camera and the uncertainties of my own insecurities. My life is one of contrasts. I observe others, and wish I could be more like them. Envy is not a trait I would gladly claim, however it exists in me. I wish I were prettier, more creative, happier.... more like someone else.

I initially entered this contest as a way to validate my worth. I continued for another purpose. Truth, perhaps? I ended up with only me.

I realized that I do have those qualities I see in others as well as the ability to cultivate them. I am creative. I am special. I am meaningful. There are intricacies of my life I thought I could not explain- and somehow I did. I learned to view myself with an architect's eye. To see the blueprints and building plans: the foundations that have turned me into who I am today.

There is a master builder who overseas these plans. God created me. I am unique. Then he gave me the blueprints and let me have creative control over the rest of my life.

On some days

remembering I am unforgettable

special
inspiring
thoughtful
good
funny
sweet
is

not so easy

day in my life

giving myself permission to ...

Relax

I am naturally a fairly high-strung person. With children to take care of and daily life, I don't have much in the way of time to relax. Even when I do manage to acquire the rare moment, I end up feeling lazy, rather than deserving of some peace and quiet.

It is okay to say NO. To take it easy. If I keep repeating it, maybe I'll end up believing it! I am guilty. If someone is upset, it must be at me. I am indecisively guilty. Decisions are hard for me. I feel guilty for feeling guilty. Do you see the vicious cycle here? The truth is I come from a long line of "guilty parties" and it is part of who I am. I give myself permission to say NO - to come to a decision - to ease my guilt. It's time for me to relax!

11/03

R E L A X

I make wrong decisions. I have regrets, and yet I continue to renovate and press forward. This home and life I am building has a greater purpose. One I am only beginning to see.

I am more than the sum of my parts. I too have a history - A history behind me, and an unknown history before me. Characteristics are bonded to the framework of my life. I will exist peacefully- unassumingly. And someday, children, grandchildren, friends, and perhaps observant strangers will enter my life, walk along my hallways and find the comforts they are looking for.

The patience of a well lived life whispers softly. Can you hear it?

Welcome home.

The farther backwards you can look, the farther forward you are likely to see.

-Sir Winston Churchill

my
grandfather
life stories

My Grandfather, G.C. Bird, means so much to me. He is not only my grandfather, but has been a second father to me.

I lived next door to him for 19 years. He has helped my own father and mother raise me to adulthood.

Anytime I had a question about anything, he was the one I'd ask. I thought he knew everything.

There were many times we'd sit up until late and talk about spiritual matters. He helped me gain the testimony I have today.

Anytime I needed a blessing, he'd either give me one or assist my father in giving me one.

He has come across as a grumpy old man, but I have always known better. I've seen many times the twinkle in his eye as he was trying to be tough with one of his grandchildren. He loves his family very much, and supports us in everything we do.

He has started to write his life story, compiled of short stories. So, I have decided to create an album, comprised of his life stories.

I love my grandfather, and I am proud of his life and the wonderful person he has come.

~Brianna Kirkham 11.13.03

my grandfather and me

Born October 14, 1931

G.C. Bird

Youngest of eleven children

Honest ★ Kind ★ Intelligent ★ Trustworthy ★

Loyal ★ Spiritual

In Celebration of My Grandfather's Life

I chose to celebrate my grandfather, G.C. Bird. He means so much to me. He is a great example of hard work, and determination. He has had a hard, but rewarding life, and I feel his story should be told.

I grew up next door to my grandfather, where he helped my parents raise me to adulthood. He disciplined me when I got out of hand. He'd sit me down and have a "talk" with me. Sometimes, when I'd really get out of hand, he'd call my parents and send me home so they could ground me. Disappointing him was enough to teach me a lesson. I looked up to my grandpa Bird.

One of the many things he taught me was how to use the wood shop. I remember spending an entire week making wooden shoes. As he helped me find the proper carving tools, I'm sure he thought that some of my ideas were silly to make, but he never would say a word.

My grandfather supports me in all I do. He and my grandmother come to all of my activities I'm involved with. He'd come to softball games, pageants, high school assemblies, dance, and piano recitals. I know that my grandfather is proud of me; he tells me in what he says and does.

Some of the fondest memories I have of my grandfather are the countless hours we'd spend talking about religious matters. If I had a question he'd not only answer it, he would help me look up the answer in a variety of religious books. He has assisted in, and gave me several Priesthood blessings. He has helped me build my testimony. He's always said, "Brianna, you'll just have to figure it out yourself."

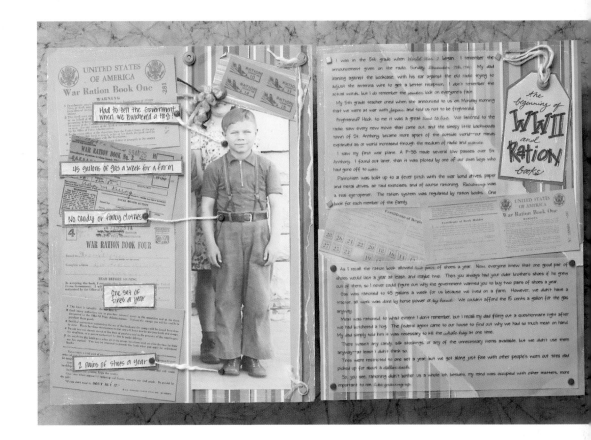

He's had a hard, but rewarding life. He is the youngest of eleven children. He was raised in a time when children were to be seen and not heard. So he wasn't heard from much, and no one paid very much attention to him. His mother died when he was 13. His father left and sold the house and farm underneath him, so he was on his own. He had to work hard to get a roof over his head. He joined the Air Force, which wasn't easy. And he has been battling a bad heart for many years.

When I was 15 years old, my grandfather had a horrible heart attack. My mother and I were the first ones there. While she called the Quick Response Unit, I called my grandma at work. I'll never forget that day. The Q.R.U. rushed him to the hospital. They prepared him for surgery. It was hard for me to see my grandfather lying there helpless on the hospital bed. It really made me realize how much he meant to me, and how much I'd need and miss him if he moved on.

He ended up surviving a 6-bypass heart surgery. He is now 72 years old. He has 6 children, 22 grandchildren, and 8 great grandchildren. He loves, and enjoys each of them very much. You can see it in his eyes as they enter the room.

Now that I am married and have my own children, I try to visit him every chance I get. I love my grandfather, and this is why I chose to create this album of his life. My hope is that he will continue to live a life of happiness, and that his posterity will draw closer to him through this album.

I knew *beyond a* doubt *that I was watching my future* WIFE

The summer before I turned 18 years old, I was in Idaho Falls, we were sitting in Anola's [my sister] living room when I walked into the kitchen and saw JoAnn walking in front of the house. As I stood there watching her, a thought came into my mind so clear and with such force that it shocked me. I knew beyond a doubt that I was watching my future wife—the mother of my children, for you see it had been revealed to me just as God lives and Jesus is the Christ.

STOP

To
nettie joann
williams

Gë & JoAnn
Forever

February
20th
1953

I Joined

Simple *times*

In July 1949, [my brother] Randie decided to re-enlist in the Air Force. I rode with him to Idaho Falls. I went to the Air Force Recruiter's office with Randie, and while he was filling out his paperwork, the Air Force Sergeant dropped a bundle of papers in front of me, pointed to them and said, "If you haven't got anything better to do, fill them out and sign them." So there it was, and I really didn't have anything else to do. No plans, no home, no future in being a farm hand, no one would miss me, so why not. I signed.

After 13 weeks of basic training, I was sent to Keesler Air Force base, Mississippi to become a control tower operator.

1949 a/c approach controller

the AIRFORCE

elizabeth chub alfred Anola Randie alphea

From the time I was very young, I learned that there were few that I could do and what I could not do, and I was raised with a strong sense on right and wrong.

There was no money for toys, and you could not buy new. You never indulged to another that you were hungry. You were respectful of everyone, even if it were old and ugly, and smelled bad.

When I was 7 years old my father started a partnership with "Babe" Worrick, a distant relative who also lived in St. Anthony. The rest of them got together, and put together a ice mill on Anthony Fill.

The mill was a beehive of activity, and nobody had time for two little people, so much to our delight, Anola and I were left to ourselves.

We spent the summer roaming the hills close by, playing on the flat, catching lizards, and anything to occupy our time.

We spent one whole day picking a quart can of wild strawberries which we sold to one of the mill hands for a dime. This was a real deal, so both got a nickel and we were rich. Mom didn't see the humor in it though and seemed to be a little irritated. Later, we earned another dime by washing the window of the cook house, and when a pie was put on the window sill, all we had to do was deliver the pie to Vic and Bill to their shanty. I didn't know what all the fuss was about that afternoon-everyone was running for Vic and Bill- but this may was good huckleberry pie.

We had a complete, every Friday night. The whole camp was there, and any other people that were around. We had hamburgers and hot dogs and all kinds of goodies.

We play-ed games, sang and told stories. Mother gathered roots and herbs and made medicine for those occasions. Many times I saw her cream off the flats with her apron full of various roots, herbs, etc. How anything that looked that bad could taste so good, I could never understand.

In the early spring Vic and Bill carressed a snow drift with sawdust, so when we wanted of ice cream, mother got together the homemade milk, we dug down through the sawdust and filled a wash tube with snow. The men was put in a gallon bucket and placed in the snow. It was our job to turn the bucket by the bail back and forth in the snow. This ice cream formed and froze up the side of the bucket. Primitive, but effective, and it sure helped to make the most of our Friday night campfires.

Samantha Walker

The Summer Of 2003

Recently, I collected a stack of pictures and mementos from my last summer and knew I wanted to do something special with them. I was having a once in a lifetime kind of summer full of fun trips and special family events. I put this album together to reflect upon a season of details to help me remember how good life is.

Since there were so many people involved in the events of my summer, I wanted to assure that my posterity would be able to follow the stories easily. That is why I started every trip with a page detailing the "cast." These will be fun pages to reflect upon. Future viewers will be able to see the ages of all the participants at the time of the events.

As I sorted through my photos, the story wrote itself. Details unfolded. I would be writing the main story and then remember a fun "inside story" about one of the "cast" members. I did not force myself to stick to a formal format, and allowed my thoughts to flow freely along many different tangents. I wrote about my in-laws and how they've affected my life, I wrote about my family and some of our funny quirks, I was able to write my testimony of my faith in Jesus Christ, I was able to write about how I love my husband and son, and able to pay tribute to the house where my husband grew up, amongst many other things. I collected letters from family members who gave new dimension to the album. Their thoughts reached deep into my heart.

My album has already started to touch the hearts of my family enabling them to see, read, touch, and feel the events. This means a lot to me because its purpose is already coming to fruition. Being able to paint these memories for my future makes this album meaningful to me.

We all come from the past, and
children ought to know that life
is a braided cord of humanity
stretching up from time long gone,
and that it can not be defined by
the span of a single journey from
diaper to shroud.

-Russel Baker

CHATTER
B·O·X

MAKE IT MEANINGFUL.

Aloha